Getting To Know...

Nature's Children

PUFFINS

Elizabeth MacLeod

SCHOLASTIC INC.

New York   Toronto   London   Auckland   Sydney
Mexico City   New Delhi   Hong Kong   Buenos Aires

FACTS IN BRIEF

Classification of Puffins

Class: *Aves* (birds)
Order: *Charadriiformes* (birds that live in ravines or cliffs)
Family: *Alcidae* (auk)
Genus: *Fratercula, Lunda*
Species: *Fratercula arctica* (Common Puffin)
Fratercula corniculata (Horned Puffin)
Lunda cirrhata (Tufted Puffin)

World distribution. North Pacific and North Atlantic oceans.

Habitat. Oceans, coastlines and islands.

Distinctive physical characteristics. Most have a black back and head with a white chest and cheeks. The triangular bill is brightly colored during the breeding season as are the legs and feet. Each foot has three toes, which are webbed.

Habits. Puffins are excellent swimmers. They winter on the ocean and return to rocky coasts or islands to breed in the spring.

Diet. Small fish, crustaceans and plankton.

Published by Scholastic Inc.
90 Old Sherman Turnpike, Danbury, Connecticut 06816.

SCHOLASTIC and associated logos are trademarks of Scholastic Inc.

ISBN 0-7172-6702-4

Printed in the U.S.A.

Have you ever wondered . . .

What looks like a cross between a penguin and a parrot? If you guessed a puffin, you're right. With their black and white feathers and colorful triangular beaks puffins are very unusual-looking birds. Although you might laugh if you saw them waddling upright on land, you would be astonished at how graceful and powerful they are swimming underwater.

Some people call puffins sea parrots or bottlenoses, but whatever you know them as, they are incredible birds. For instance, did you know that a puffin has its brightly colored beak for only a few months of the year? Or that most puffins prefer to nest underground?

To find out more about these special birds, read on.

A Family of Divers

Puffins are members of the auk family, a group of diving sea birds with short tails and necks. Birds in this family are strong swimmers, and include auklets, murres, guillemots and razorbills, as well as the Great Auk — a large flightless bird that is now extinct. A puffin's more distant cousins are sandpipers, gulls and plovers. Even though puffins look like small penguins, they're not related.

If you compare a puffin's foot — or the foot of any bird in the same family — to just about any other bird's foot, you'll see that they look different. Birds in the auk family have only three toes, whereas most birds have a fourth toe that faces backwards. This is just one of the things that sets puffins apart.

A Common, or Atlantic Puffin.

Three's Company

There are three kinds of puffins. At first glance you might think that they are all quite similar, but take a closer look and you'll see that it's not all that difficult to tell them apart.

The Common, or Atlantic, Puffin is probably the one that you've seen most often in photographs. It has a big bright bill, a black back and white chest feathers. It's the smallest of the three puffins and it nests on coastlines along the Atlantic Ocean, from Greenland down to northern Maine in the United States. It can also be found on the coasts of Iceland, Ireland, France and along the north coast of the Soviet Union.

The biggest puffin is the Tufted Puffin. Even though it's the largest, it only weighs a little more than a loaf of bread and stands about as high as your knee. It gets its name from the tufts of yellow feathers on the sides of its head. These tufts look quite handsome as they stream out behind the puffin when it flies. However, when the Tufted Puffin is perched on a rock, the wind can blow the long feathers all over its face, making it difficult for the poor bird to see. You'll find this puffin along the Pacific coastline from Alaska to California, as well as in Japan.

The Horned Puffin is the middle-sized puffin. If you notice the fleshy "horn" by its eye, you'll know how it gets its name. It nests on the west coast of North America and the east coast of Asia.

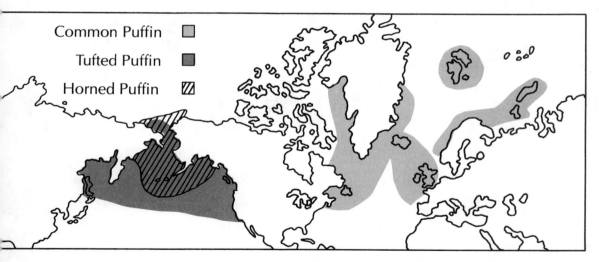

Where puffins nest and feed.

Below the Waves

Puffins are expert divers and swimmers. They don't look very dynamic as they bob along the ocean's surface, but the instant they spot a school of fish far below, they flick their wings open and go into action. With just one powerful stroke and a back kick, they're underwater. Then they partially fold back their wings and use them as propellers. Like penguins, puffins seem to fly, not swim, through the water. They zoom along just as most birds move through the air. To glide, a puffin simply pulls its wings in close to its body.

Notice how streamlined this puffin looks whizzing through the water.

Fish Lovers

Puffins dine upon crab, plankton, squid and fish, with smelt, herring, cod and sand eels being their favorites.

You may have seen a picture of a puffin with a beak filled with fish. Just how does it manage to fit as many as 40 small fish in its beak at the same time? By catching them in a special way.

As this fabulous fisherman swims underwater through a school of fish, it moves its head from side to side. This allows the puffin to stack the fish one at a time crosswise in its bill. Tiny spines on its tongue and the upper part of its beak hold the catch firmly in place. Once its beak is filled, the puffin flies up out of the water to a nearby cliff or island to feed its young.

When a puffin is dining alone, it doesn't stack fish. Instead it simply eats them as it catches them.

A beakful of fish to feed its offspring.

Eye Spy

Have you ever noticed how difficult it is for you to see things clearly when you dive underwater? That's because your eyes are designed to see well in air. Since you don't spend a lot of time underwater, it's not important that you see well there. But puffins have to be eagle-eyed in air and in water.

Fortunately, puffins — like all birds — have an extra set of eyelids. The middle part of these eyelids is clear, and the puffin simply flicks them across its eyes when it dives underwater. The eyelids act like goggles keeping the water from blurring the puffin's vision and enabling it to spot a likely meal.

The fleshy "horn" of this Horned Puffin makes its eyes appear larger than they really are.

Waterproof Feathers

A puffin depends on its brilliant black and white feathers to keep it warm and dry, no matter how long it stays underwater. To keep its coat in shape it spends a lot of time preening.

First the puffin ruffles its feathers and removes any damaged ones. Then it spreads oil from a gland near its tail all over its feathers. The oil provides a waterproof coating and also helps to keep the feathers properly arranged. Hooks or barbs on the feathers lock them together, making the puffin as streamlined as possible so that it can fly through the air or swim through the water smoothly.

Taking off with a lot of splashing.

Up, Up and Away

Puffins are fairly good fliers but they do have trouble with their take-offs and landings. Because of their relatively small wings and chunky bodies, they have to beat their wings very fast to lift off. Sometimes if they're taking off from the water, they end up crashing headfirst into the waves. Luckily puffins are so tough that they bob up safely or bounce into the air. Taking off is a lot easier if they launch themselves from cliffs.

When it's time to land a puffin seems to have very little control. To slow down, it spreads it feet in front of itself and flares its tail. It also helps if the bird can touch down with the wind blowing into its face. However, unlike most birds which coast to a stop, puffins appear to just drop in. When they land on water you'll even hear a loud plop. On land, any puffins standing around watch nervously and get ready to scatter when another comes in for a landing.

Three, two, one . . . blast-off!

Brrr!

Imagine going through the whole winter floating about on the cold ocean, spending your days diving and dozing. That's what puffins seem to do. From approximately September to March each year they swim about catching fish, usually with only a few other puffins for company.

Actually, scientists aren't absolutely sure what puffins do all winter or exactly where they go. Most experts think that the birds scatter widely over the ocean and never come ashore at all during the winter months. Some may spend the cold months very close to their summer nesting grounds, while others may migrate long distances. Wherever they do go, they are rarely within sight of land for the entire winter.

A Tufted Puffin.

Creaks, Purrs and Gurgles

A puffin makes a lot of different sounds. If it wants to threaten another puffin — or some other bird — it lets out a short, harsh *urrr* sound. It also communicates by making a deep, purring *arrr* and a short *haa-haa* laugh. While sitting on its egg, a parent may make a long call that sounds like *haa-aa-aa-aa*.

Puffins also get their point across without making any noise at all. They greet one another by standing face to face, with one's bill on top of the other's, and pushing back and forth like a seesaw. A big, wide-mouthed yawn tells other puffins to stay away. Sometimes this yawn follows a sound like a rusty hinge creaking or a gurgle.

When two puffins get into a fight, they growl, trying to scare each other off. If that doesn't work, one will grab the other's jaw with its bill, then the two roll about, slashing with their wings and feet. They can become so involved in their fight that they may even roll over the edge of a cliff!

"Are you friend or foe?"

Look Out!

Puffins nest on islands or on rocky cliffs overlooking the sea. Although there aren't many other animals in these places, they still have to be on the lookout for predators. Ravens, gulls, peregrine falcons, crows and eagles all hunt puffins, and puffins that nest in northern areas have to beware of snowy owls as well. Most of these birds will also steal food from adult puffins and try to fly off with eggs or chicks. Foxes, river otters and rats can also be a danger since they consider puffin eggs a tasty treat.

Waiting for the fog to lift.

All Together

Puffins nest in large groups known as colonies. There may be as many as 50,000 birds in a single colony. Horned Puffins and Tufted Puffins sometimes nest in the same areas and compete with each other for burrows. Other birds, such as petrels, terns and guillemots, may also share the same locations.

No matter how closely packed together puffins are, they defend their tiny territories fiercely, and the colonies can become very noisy as the birds squawk and scream at one another. Living in a group has its advantages, however. For instance, it's easy to find out where the fish are just by watching where the other birds are having luck fishing.

Busy Beak

Puffins' beaks are useful for a lot more than just catching and carrying food. During the mating season they come in handy as shovels or chisels to dig burrows in hard earth. And they can also be used as pliers to remove rocks from burrows. Sometimes these rocks weigh twice as much as the puffin!

Puffins also use their beaks to attract a mate. Most of the year the beak is small and a dull gray-brown color. During the breeding season, however, the bill grows a brightly colored sheath that makes it twice its usual size.

After the mating season, this brilliant sheath falls off in sections. The Tufted Puffin, for example, drops its beak cover in seven pieces.

The bright colors of this puffin's beak will surely help it to attract a mate.

Paddles and Diggers

Puffins have an amazing number of uses for their big webbed feet. Naturally, they use them to scramble over the rocky shores where they nest and to paddle as they float on the ocean's waves. They also use them to steer when they dive deep underwater, and to help dig their burrows.

Puffin foot showing claws.

Each toe ends in a sharp claw which helps the puffin grab on and keep its balance as it climbs over rocks and stones. A strong, curved, sharp inner toenail on each foot works as a pick to help the bird dig in the hard, rocky soil where it makes its nest. And the webbing between its toes makes it easy for the puffin to toss the soil out behind it as it works.

Just like the puffin's beak, its feet become very colorful during the mating season. They turn from brownish-green to bright red to help the puffin look its best to attract a mate.

Mating Time

By the time the mating season comes around, both the male and female puffins have grown their large, colorful beaks and their feet have become brightly colored as well. Puffin courtship takes place on land and in the water. It usually begins on a cliff when a young male spots an unattached young female. He walks over to her and nibbles lightly at her bill. If she's interested she stands facing him, chest to chest, and they shake their heads rapidly so that their bills clash. Afterwards they may run around each other, then crouch and nuzzle each other's bill. Then they take to the sea, calling and diving and rubbing bills.

Courtship is very important to puffins because they usually mate for life. The courtship process lasts from two to seven days, during which the birds nuzzle each other's throats and chest feathers, nod their heads and give their mating call. The male may also open his mouth and display the brightly colored insides.

"Back off – this is our territory!"

Home Sweet Home

Once a puffin has chosen a mate, the pair finds a suitable spot to nest. Older puffins may return to the same nest year after year. A new pair will try to find a burrow that was dug by some other bird, or by a rabbit. If necessary, they'll dig their own.

The nest is a tunnel about a metre (3 feet) long, often curved down to about 30 centimetres (a foot) below the surface. Burrows may be connected underground, but each one has a private entrance and a nest chamber at the end of the tunnel. Sometimes a burrow will have two "tenants" since other seabirds, such as razorbills or guillemots, may nest just inside the entrance to the tunnel.

The puffins carry grass, seaweed and feathers into the nest burrow and drop the materials anywhere in the passageway. There's no proper lining to soften the inside of the rocky tunnel or protect the egg that will soon be laid there.

A little foliage to make the burrow more homey.

Countdown

The female puffin usually lays one egg. She may lay a second egg later if something happens to the first one. The egg is white with light purple or brown spots at its large end. Both parents take turns sitting on the egg and since it's fairly big, the parent has to tuck it under one wing and lean his or her body on it to keep it warm. Both parents have special spots under each wing just for incubating eggs.

The parents take turns keeping the egg warm, although the female does most of the work. She spends long periods on the egg, usually changing places with her mate for a while at night. By the beginning of July, about 42 days after it was laid, the egg is ready to hatch.

Guarding the entrance to a burrow.

Welcome to the World

It takes the baby puffin about four days to break out of its shell. When it finally emerges, the baby is covered in soft down and doesn't look much like its parents at all. For the first few days the parents stay with the hatchling almost continually and take turns catching fish for it.

The chick starts right off eating small fish without needing to have them predigested by its parents. It can eat its entire weight in fish each day, and the parents make as many as eight flights a day to get it food. During the 40 to 45 days the chick stays in the burrow, it may consume up to 2000 fish!

This fluffy puffball doesn't look the least bit like its parents.

A Jump in the Dark

By the time the baby puffin is about six weeks old it looks quite similar to its parents, although its bill is small and dark and its wings are not yet fully developed. At this point its mom and dad leave it and return to the water. Their feathers are ready to molt and they will be unable to fly for several weeks until their new feathers grow in. They are therefore no longer able to carry fish from the ocean to the cliff for their offspring.

The chick may sit in the burrow for up to a week waiting for its parents to return. Finally, once its flight feathers have grown in, it decides it's ready to find out what's outside the tunnel.

Chicks usually leave their nests at night, which is a good thing because that makes it more difficult for enemies to spot them. The little puffins tumble over the sides of the cliffs to the water below. Don't worry, they're very light and fluffy, and they always land safely. After a quick shake of their feathers they're soon swimming. They seem to know instinctively how to dive for food, and in a few days they begin to fly.

Opposite page:
The world beyond the burrow can be a frightening place.

43

All Grown Up

Scientists can't seem to agree on whether young puffins find their parents in the ocean and spend the winter with them or not. It seems unlikely. What we do know is that the youngsters remain on the ocean for two years and don't head back to land until their second or third summer. Talk about a lot of swimming!

At the age of about three the young puffin arrives at the breeding spot early and tries to find a mate and a burrow. It may not succeed for another year or two, however. By that time it is a full-grown puffin and has learned everything it needs to know to raise a family. With a little luck, it may live for another 15 years in the northern oceans of the world.

Time to return to the sea for winter.

Words to Know

Breeding season   The time of year during which animals come together to produce young.

Chick   A young bird before or after hatching.

Colony   Name given to the large groups in which puffins nest.

Down   Short, soft feathers that cover young birds or underlie the outer feathers of adult birds.

Hatch   To emerge from an egg.

Hatchling   A chick that is breaking out or has just broken out of the egg.

Migrate   To move from one place to another regularly, according to the season.

Molt   To shed feathers, skin, shell or horns periodically before a new growth.

Plankton   Very small animal or plant life that lives near the surface of salt and fresh water.

Predator   An animal that hunts other animals for food.

Preening   Cleaning and oiling the feathers.

Smelt   Small green and silver fish.

Territory   Area that an animal or group of animals lives in and often defends from other animals of the same kind.

INDEX

Cover Photo: A. Petretti (WWF–Photolibrary)

Photo Credits: Breck P. Kent, pages 4, 13, 34-35; Brenda Tharp, pages 6, 30; New York Zoological Society, page 10; Derek Kirkland (Network Stock Photo File), page 14; Barry Griffiths (Network Stock Photo File), pages 17, 26, 29, 33, 38; Cynthia and Amor Klotzbach, pages 18, 45; Boyd Norton, page 21; G. Ziesler (Peter Arnold, Inc.), page 23; G.C. Kelley, pages 24, 42; Phyllis Greenberg, pages 37, 46; Bruno J. Zehnder (Peter Arnold, Inc.), page 41.

Getting To Know...

Nature's Children

OLD WORLD MONKEYS

Bill Ivy

SCHOLASTIC INC.

New York   Toronto   London   Auckland   Sydney
Mexico City   New Delhi   Hong Kong   Buenos Aires

FACTS IN BRIEF

Classification of Old World Monkeys

Class:	*Mammalia* (mammals)
Order:	*Primates* (monkeys, apes, lemurs, people)
Family:	*Cercopithecidae*
Subfamilies:	*Cercopithecinae* (monkeys with cheek pouches)
	Colobinae (leaf monkeys)
Genus:	There are 12 genera of Old World Monkeys.
Species:	There are over 70 species of Old World Monkeys.

World distribution.   Africa, India, China, Japan and Southeast Asia.

Habitat.   Varies with species.

Distinctive physical characteristics.   Most species have arms and legs of equal length, opposable thumbs and big toes, and a long tail. The nostrils are curved, close together and open downwards. There are thick calluses on the buttocks.

Habits.   Live in communities of 4 to 100. Most sleep in trees at night. Mainly active during the day.

Diet.   Varies with species.

Published by Scholastic Inc.
90 Old Sherman Turnpike, Danbury, Connecticut 06816.

SCHOLASTIC and associated logos are trademarks of Scholastic Inc.

ISBN 0-7172-6702-4

Printed in the U.S.A.

Have you ever wondered . . .

Which animals do you think are the most popular ones at the zoo? Probably the monkeys and for good reason. With their expressive faces and humorous antics they often remind us of mischievous little people. In fact, when people play pranks we may say they are up to "monkey business" and when we are teased by our friends we may tell them to stop "monkeying around."

Monkeys are not only playful, they are curious, noisy, intelligent and they're great acrobats as well. People have always been fascinated by them and in some countries monkeys are considered sacred.

Want to have more fun than a barrel of monkeys? Then turn the page and learn more about these incredible animals.

Barbary macaque.

Old or New

Most monkeys live in the tropics where the weather is always warm but a few live in areas where the winters are very cold. Scientists divide monkeys into two groups. Those that live in Central and South America are called New World monkeys, while those found in Africa and Asia are called Old World monkeys.

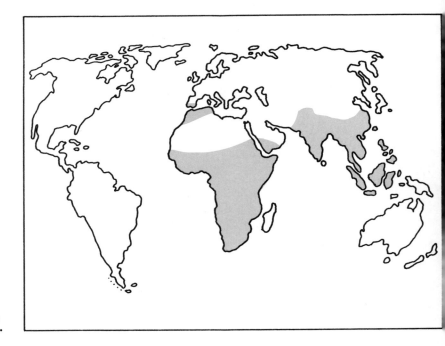

The shaded areas on this map show where Old World monkeys are found.

There are several ways to tell which group a particular monkey belongs to even if you don't know where it came from. If the monkey has a prehensile, or grasping, tail and can use it as an extra hand for picking up things or swinging from trees, it is a New World monkey. No Old World monkey can do these things with its tail. You can also tell by looking closely at the monkey's face. Old World monkeys have nostrils that are close together and open towards the front. The nostrils of a New World monkey are wide, round, and further apart, and they open to the sides.

Only Old World monkeys have their own handy seat cushions, pads of tough skin on their bottom to make sitting more comfortable. Some also have cheek pouches for storing food. And many Old World monkeys have something else very special that New World monkeys don't — opposable thumbs just like yours.

Black-tailed marmoset
NEW WORLD

De Brazza's monkey
OLD WORLD

Thumbs Up

Take a close look at one of your hands and pick something up. Did you notice how you used your thumb and fingers together? Now try it again only this time without using your thumb. Not so easy, is it? We are able to move our thumb around to meet our fingers so we are said to have opposable thumbs.

Many Old World monkeys also have opposable thumbs. But they have something we don't have — opposable big toes! This means they can pick up objects as easily with their feet as they can with their hands. And these special toes and thumbs are very useful for climbing trees, swinging from branch to branch, peeling fruit and just about everything else.

Macaque hand

The hand of the lion-tailed macaque is very similar to your own, nails and all.

Real Troopers

Opposite page:
A troop of olive baboons on the move.

Monkeys, like apes, lemurs and people, are primates. Old World monkeys are strong, agile animals with long limbs. In fact, their arms are about the same length as their legs, which helps them to be great climbers and also fast runners on all fours. Their tail varies from a mere stub to an elegant plume longer than their body. Their size ranges from the tiny talapoin, which weighs about a kilogram (2.2 pounds), to the mighty baboon, which may tip the scales at 45 kilograms (100 pounds).

Monkeys enjoy each other's company and rarely live alone. Some stay in pairs but most gather in groups known as troops. A troop may contain anywhere from 4 to over 100 individuals. Often one male plus several females and their young make up a troop.

High up in the trees monkeys have few enemies. While an occasional owl or hawk may attack a youngster, their main concern is other primates. However, those species that spend a lot of time on the ground have to be on the lookout for animals such as cheetahs, lions and jackals.

Monkey Sense

All monkeys are intelligent, but the Old World species are believed to be even brighter than their New World relatives. Apparently they rely less on instinct and more on reason. And they have an excellent memory, remembering from season to season where their favorite trees are and exactly when the fruit will be ripe.

Monkeys have very good eyesight and it's a good thing they do: leaping from branch to branch and being short-sighted could be quite a problem. Many mammals see the world in shades of gray, but monkeys see in color just as we do, and most of them see better in daylight than at night. Their sense of smell is good but not as keen as that of many other animals. They rely on their eyes more than their nose to find food. Since they have such small ears they often have to turn their head from side to side to zero in on sounds.

The Japanese macacque is known for its inventiveness as well as for its ability to withstand bitterly cold winters.

On the Menu

Many people think monkeys live mainly on bananas, but actually they eat an incredible variety of food. Here is a list of some of their favorite things: fruit, nuts, seeds, leaves, tubers, flowers, insects, spiders, crabs and birds' eggs. Some even eat small mammals. Many species live almost entirely on leaves. With their agile hands they have no trouble peeling fruit or removing bark from trees to find the juicy insects underneath. Of course monkeys also need water to live and most drink by drawing in water with their lips. A few, however, lap up water like a dog.

Monkeys must find fresh food each day since they store only what they can hold in their cheeks. Cheek pouches actually extend below the jaws and can pack quite a bit of food — possibly as much as a stomachful for some species.

One hand for food still leaves one for cuddling the baby. (Vervet monkeys)

Chitter Chatter

Monkeys talk to each other but not in words as we do. Instead they use a variety of different sounds, depending on whether they are happy, angry or afraid. Their most common call is a rapid chattering. When they are angry they shriek and scold each other. The loud call of the male rallies the rest of the troop together, warns of danger and lets other groups in the area know where he is and who's in charge.

Because monkeys have such expressive faces it is easy to tell what kind of mood they are in. Whether they are curious, content, happy or excited, you can see it on their faces. When it is angry a monkey pulls back its lips and shows its teeth. When it is tired or bored it lets out a big yawn.

*When a male hamadryas baboon shows his teeth, he **really** has something to show.*

Grooming Parties

Do you enjoy having your hair washed, dried and brushed? Many people find this relaxing. For monkeys, having their coat groomed is just as enjoyable, and it's helpful too. They spend a lot of time carefully removing dirt and insects from each other's hair, using their hands and often their teeth as well. Social standing in the troop determines who grooms who. Friends of equal status groom each other, while a male leader may have many lower ranking members wanting to groom him. Mothers and other females often groom the young ones.

Monkeys groom each other not only to rid themselves of pests, but often just for fun. In the same way that we like to visit with our friends, monkeys like to get together for a grooming party. It helps to calm them down and is probably a way of showing affection and friendship.

"Where on earth did you pick this up?" (Mandrills)

I'm All Ears

By the time most monkeys are four or five years old they are ready to start a family. Females mate with the leader of the troop to make sure they have the strongest, healthiest father for their offspring. Young males usually have to fight with older males for the chance to mate with females in the troop. Often it takes a male quite some time and many attempts at a number of troops before he wins a mate.

About six months after mating the female gives birth to a single infant — in rare cases twins. She usually has her baby at night high up in a tree. She does not make a nest or prepare any type of nursery. Immediately after birth the wide-eyed and alert youngster clings to the fur on its mother's belly. If it cannot support its own weight the mother will put her hand on its back for extra support. She also gives her baby its first bath by licking it clean.

Except for being able to grab hold, a newborn monkey is totally helpless. It is covered in soft velvety fur which is often a different color than that of its parents.

Opposite page:
Like most baby monkeys, this young hamadryas baboon has ears that seem way too big for its head.

Monkey See, Monkey Do

For the first few days of its life the newborn monkey spends its time sleeping and nursing on its mother's milk. It will be at least six months to a year before it will be weaned. In at least one species the baby monkey sucks its thumb.

In some families the father helps to look after his offspring and may even carry it around. Sometimes other members of the troop babysit the youngster. But no matter who is helping out, the mother keeps a watchful eye and ear out for her baby and will return to its side at the least sign of trouble.

By the third month the young monkey's coat is gradually replaced by a new fluffier one which is similar to its parents' fur but not as clearly marked. By this time too, the youngster has begun to learn by copying what its mother does. When mother and child go off looking for food, the young monkey eats the same things it sees her eating. Soon it knows what's good to eat and what isn't.

This baby silvered langur's spectacular orange coat will last only a few months.

Monkeying Around

Young monkeys are very active and love to play. They chase each other, wrestle and scamper up and down trees. Two of their favorite games are follow the leader and king of the castle. Sometimes they even tease their mother by swinging on her tail! Luckily for them adult monkeys are usually very patient and will put up with a lot of "monkey business." Playing is not only fun but it helps to make them good climbers and teaches them to get along with others, which is very important in a monkey troop.

Monkeys mature more slowly than other animals their size. The bond between mothers and daughters lasts into adulthood, and females often stay in the troop they were born into. Males, on the other hand, often leave and join other young males in a temporary bachelor group while they wait till they are able to join a new troop.

Caught in the act!

Colorful Coats

In Africa the most common monkeys are the guenons. Most of them live high up in trees, seldom coming down to the ground. The main exceptions are the different types of green monkeys, who nest and take refuge in trees but spend most of their time on the ground.

All guenons have tails longer than their bodies and cheek pouches in which they store food they don't want to eat right away. Guenons are very handsome monkeys about the size of a housecat. Many have brightly colored coats with bold, contrasting patterns. Mustaches, beards and striped sideburns are also common, especially in the males. Their names — red-eared, owl-faced, white-nosed — give you some idea of what they look like. Guenons are quite tolerant of each other and in some areas several different species live happily side by side.

De Brazza's monkey.

Lanky Langurs

Lanky, lean, graceful, these are a few words that describe the langur monkeys of India and parts of the Far East. There are more than 50 different kinds and they come in a variety of sizes, shapes and colors. Some live in forests while others brave the chilly slopes of the Himalaya mountains. They are primarily leaf-eaters and have a special digestive system similar to that of a cow which helps them get as much nourishment as possible from their food.

Most langurs spend the majority of their time in trees. However, the gray or Hanuman langur is mainly a ground dweller. This langur is considered sacred in parts of India and is protected by law, free to roam the countryside and even city streets as it pleases. It is an adaptable monkey that lives in woodlands, forests and farmlands.

The handsome Hanuman.

Super Snout

Meet the Pinocchio of the monkey world, the proboscis monkey. The word proboscis means "long flexible snout" so it's no mystery how this comical-looking monkey got its name. Both the males and the females have long noses but the male's is sometimes so long it hangs below his chin. And the bigger the male's nose is, the more attractive females find him. This super snout is not just there for looks, however; it serves as a loudspeaker when the male gives his loud *honk-keehonk* warning call.

The proboscis monkey is found in swampy forests on the island of Borneo. Leaves make up the bulk of its diet and it spends a good part of the day resting between meals. It can be surprisingly active when it wants to, though. Despite its large size — up to 23 kilograms (52 pounds) for a male — it is an excellent climber. It is also a daring high diver and often jumps from trees into water over 15 metres (50 feet) below — and then dogpaddles away with ease. The proboscis monkey has a nose for trouble and when threatened will dive and swim underwater.

Opposite page:
Rather surprisingly, the super-sized nose of the proboscis monkey does not seem to give it a better sense of smell than other monkeys have.

Mangabey Monkeys

Mangabey monkeys live mainly in the forests of West and Central Africa. They come in a variety of colors but all have white upper eyelids that can been seen from great distances. They are slender, long-tailed animals weighing from 3 to 12 kilograms (7 to 26 pounds).

The deep grunting call of the gray-cheeked mangabey sounds like a "hesitant turkey with a frog in its throat." It is a rather noisy monkey that can often be heard high in treetops ripping a meal of bark from trees. It also eats fruit, flowers, insects and birds' eggs, and will bite the head off a snake before eating the rest of it. Gray-cheeked mangabeys have a larger home range than most forest monkeys because they are so effective at finding all available food in an area that they must wait quite a while before returning to it.

You probably won't be a bit surprised to learn that this mangabey monkey is commonly known as the red-capped mangabey.

Royal Family

Most people are familiar with the baboon, the largest of all monkeys. Males can grow to be over a metre (3 feet) tall. Females are about half that size. Baboons are known as dog-faced monkeys. Come to think of it, they do look a bit like a large poodle with their long muzzle. One species, the hamadryas baboon of Ethiopia and Arabia, is the famous sacred monkey of ancient Egypt that was often made into a mummy.

Baboons are ground dwellers and rarely climb trees except to sleep. Troops average about 40 individuals and travel 3 to 4 kilometres (2 to 2.5 miles) a day searching for food. It is believed that some baboons never move more than a metre (3 feet) away from another baboon in their entire life. Now that's togetherness!

Baboons have a reputation for being aggressive and when threatened they can indeed be very ferocious. Male baboons will fight a leopard or even a lion that threatens the troop. However, they are generally friendly and gentle with each other.

Opposite page: While the hamadryas baboon can look quite imposing, it is actually the smallest of the baboons.

Big Bold and Beautiful

Let's face it, animals don't get much more colorful than this. With its brilliant blue-ribbed cheeks, red nose and rosy bottom, the mandrill is one of a kind. The males have the brightest colors and when they get angry their face gets even more vivid. Females are not so gaudy and less than half the size of their mates.

Mandrills live in the forests of West Africa and for this reason are known as forest baboons. This is one animal you would not want to "monkey around" with. An adult male is as strong as a leopard and when threatened as powerful as a gorilla. Not to mention the fact that its canine teeth are as long as a tiger's.

Mandrills are big, measuring in at just under a metre (3 feet) tall. Their tails are short for a monkey, usually less than 10 centimetres (4 inches) long. Mandrills walk on their fingers and toes, never letting their palms touch the ground. To rest they often lean forward on their hands. They will eat almost anything, and when water is scarce they dig in the bottom of dry riverbeds to find it.

Fleet of Foot

If all the primates in the world were to have a race, no one would be able to keep up with the patas monkey. This streamlined, long-legged animal is built like a greyhound. With its bounding gait it can reach speeds of up to 55 kilometres (34 miles) an hour. The patas monkey lives in the savannah regions of Africa. Although it is a ground dweller it will often climb a small tree to find food or to take a quick look around. It also sleeps in trees at night.

The patas monkey belongs to the same family as do the guenons. With its reddish coat and its white mustache, it is a rather dashing looking monkey. Males weigh an average of 10 kilograms (22 pounds) although some may be twice that. Females are smaller, weighing in at about 7 kilograms (15 pounds) or less. A typical troop contains 20 animals or so. Patas monkeys are relatively quiet. Even when threatened they only make soft chirping sounds.

The patas monkey is also known as the hussar or military monkey.

Aerial Acrobats

The colobus monkey has a beautiful coat of long, fine hair. While there are red and olive colobuses, most are a striking black and white.

Colobus monkeys are known as leaf monkeys because they can eat large amounts of foliage. However, some species eat more fruit and seeds than they do leaves. They live in forests in the middle of Africa high up in the treetops. Incredible acrobats, they often leap 8 metres (25 feet) or more from branch to branch. They can even change direction in mid-air! But most of the time they move rather slowly, resting between feedings, and often travel only 500 metres (yards) in a day.

Colobus monkeys are unusual because they only have a small nub of a thumb or none at all. This is how they get their name, which means docked or mutilated. Having no thumbs doesn't slow down these monkeys, though. They are very skilled at picking up things and climbing trees with only their fingers and palms.

Feeling Frosty

There are more than 15 different species of macaque monkeys in the world. With the exception of one species they all live in Asia. Most have drab brown, gray or yellow coats but some have bright colored skin on their face. Macaques are essentially ground dwellers and are very good at walking on two feet.

Two well-known members of this family are the rhesus monkey, a favorite of zoos, and the Japanese macaque. The Japanese macaque lives the farthest north of all the monkeys in the world. During the winter when snow covers the forests and mountains of Japan and there are no leaves on the trees, these thick-coated animals survive by eating bark. They keep warm by huddling together and by taking dips in nearby hot springs where they dogpaddle in the steaming water.

Japanese macaque.

Helping Out

We owe a great deal to monkeys. Not only are they fascinating to watch, they have helped us in many ways. Thanks to well-trained monkeys many disabled people now have a much needed helper in the home. These faithful companions give their owners an independence never before possible.

Did you know the first astronaut was a rhesus monkey? And that's not its only claim to fame. Thanks to research with these monkeys a vaccine for polio was discovered and many children have been spared from this disabling disease. It was also by studying rhesus monkeys that scientists identified the Rh (for rhesus) positive and negative factors that exist in our blood as well as monkeys'. This too has saved many lives.

Monkeys certainly deserve our respect and protection. It is very important that we stop destroying their forests so that these amazing animals will always have a place to live.

Words to Know

Canine tooth   One of four strong pointed teeth, located between the front teeth and the molars.

Groom   To clean or brush, especially hair.

Home range   Area where an animal lives and looks for food.

Mate   To come together to produce young. Either member of an animal pair is also the other's mate.

Opposable thumb   The kind of thumb that is separated from the fingers and can be moved around to meet them. Humans and a few animals, including Old World monkeys and chimpanzees, have opposable thumbs.

Prehensile   Adapted for grabbing and holding, especially by wrapping around an object. Many New World monkeys and some other animals, such as opossums, have prehensile tails. Old World monkeys however do not.

Primate   An animal that belongs to the order Primates, such as a monkey, chimpanzee or human being.

Proboscis   A long, flexible snout (pronounced pro.BOSS.is).

Troop   A group of monkeys that live together with the strongest male in charge.

INDEX

Cover Photo: Bill Ivy
Photo Credits: Bill Ivy, pages 4, 8, 12, 16, 20, 28, 36, 39; George Holton, page 11;
Robert Winslow, page 15; Nancy Adams, pages 19, 32, 35, 40; Fletcher & Baylis (Photo
Researchers, Inc.), page 22; Brian Vikander (West Light), pages 24, 25; Nancy Staley,
page 27; Fred Bavendam (Peter Arnold, Inc.), page 31; Gregory Dimijian (Photo
Researchers, Inc.), page 43; Akira Uchiyama (Photo Researchers, Inc.), page 45.